Book Cover Design by: Haley Sharon

Illustrations by: Haley Sharon

First Edition 2025

ISBN: 979-8-218-58319-4

Library of Congress Control Number: 2024927497

"Touch" (2021 Epilogue) [Feat. Paul Williams]
Performed By: Daft Punk,Douglas Walter,Paul Williams
Written By: Chris Caswell (ASCAP),Guy-Manuel de Homem-Christo (BMI)
Paul Williams (ASCAP),Thomas Bangalter (BMI)

"Daydream"
Performed By: Gunter Kallmann Choir
Written By: David Mckay,Pyor Ilyich Tchaikovsky, Raymond Vincent

"Fade Into You"
Performed By: Mazzy Star
Written By: David Roback,Hope Sandoval
Published By: Wixen Music Publishing, Inc. o/b/o Sand Devil Music and Wixen Music Publishing, Inc. o/b/o Salley Gardens
Publishing

"Chamber Of Reflection"
Performed By: Your Anxiety Buddy
Written By: Mac DeMarco
Published By: Secretly Canadian Publishi o/b/o Mac Demarco dba

"Landslide"
Performed By: Fleetwood Mac
Written By: Stevie Nicks
Published By: Kobalt Music Pub America I o/b/o Welsh Witch Music

3

To those who

lied

cheated

loved

stole

broke

hated

cherished

destroyed

kissed

comforted

manipulated

I would like to thank you for making me who I am today. This book is dedicated to you.

I Love you...

I do

I HATE YOU
I DO

Written By:

Adam Strohschein

Illustrations By:

Haley Sharon

"I love you, I do… I hate you, I do" is a journey through the start, middle, ending and moving on from a relationship. On certain pages you will notice a QR code, when scanned this takes you to a song to set the mood for your reading experience. If you wish to just listen to the extended playlist with songs in feel of the book it is included on this page. I would suggest saving that after reading the book with the intended songs in order. Take time with each page, read the words and imagine speaking and thinking these along with the soundtrack.

When I first met you
I needed to learn you.

You make me nervous, but in a good way.

Please don't hurt me.

Adam Strohschein

I believe I have feelings for you, but I
don't know if you feel the same.

I can't help but look at you, it's so stupid
but it makes me nervous when you look
back.

I can't do this again, can I?
what if?

I think I'm in trouble.

I find myself thinking
mostly about you,
this isn't good.

What if you hurt me?
Like the others,
what if?

I wish I knew what you were thinking.

I hate how you're always on my mind,
don't stop.

You always look so calm and relaxed.
Little do you know I'm a mess inside
because of you.

I don't know if I can do this again.

Adam Strohschein

I want to fix you,
are you as broken as me?

Give me a sign this is something.

Adam Strohschein

Just give up on love they told me.
But when one sees your face.
You can make an atheist a believer.
You shouldn't exist,
you have no reason to be here.
But here you are,
you made me a believer.
How can you be real?

You always know how to make me laugh,
even without trying. Your smile is so
warm.
I want to live there.

Hold on.

When you speak you sound like my favorite song.

Adam Strohschein

You make me want to be the best version
of myself.

I wish you'd get the courage to tell me how much you feel for me as much as I do for you.

Adam Strohschein

Maybe you're afraid as much as I am.
I know this is real,
I can feel it.

Now throughout my day everything
redirects my mind to you.

I want to read you like a book, thumb through your pages and make my way to the end, reading you cover to cover.

In my mind I have everything planned out, but I've come to expect the unexpected.

Adam Strohschein

I could be around you all the time.

You feel like home.

Being with you makes every mistake before you worth the hurt just to know you were the lead up.

I'm in trouble, like beyond the point. I wanted this for so long and now it's almost here and I have no idea how to act. I'm not even myself and I hate that. You need to see the real me, only then will I accept this. It's the last wish I need granted.

Adam Strohschein

We are two damaged people but for
different reasons.

I want to give you my everything.

Adam Strohschein

I've stared into your eyes so much if you asked me what color they are I couldn't give you an answer.

Anytime you get close to me, I can feel
my whole body get warm.

Can you feel it?

Adam Strohschein

Sometimes the suspense is unbearable
and I wonder if I can go on, but then I
see, how <u>you</u> look at me,
how <u>you</u> talk to me,
how I feel around you.

You make me crazy.

Adam Strohschein

This is the point of no return, everyone
can sense something between us and you
have to feel it.

You have to feel it,
cause everyday you're in it,
cause everyday I'm in it,
somethings gotta give.
Give into it.

I think I'm in love with you.

Adam Strohschein

Sometimes this roller coaster ride comes
to moments of clarity, and I find myself
wondering if it's all too good to be true.
Then the ride starts again, and I can't
help myself.

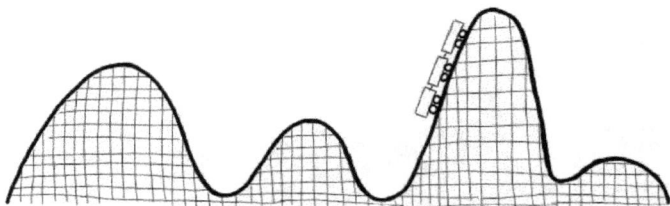

Anyone who wants to doubt this isn't something, isn't on the high I'm on now.

I enjoy the way we catch each other's attention and laugh.

I have the biggest smile all the time.

Adam Strohschein

It feels like everything depends on this very moment, I want my timing to be perfect. So here I sit waiting, all the while you have absolutely no clue. You have to sense it... ok I'm ready.

I don't know what to say, it finally
happened, it's everything I could have
imagined and more.
It's so hard to explain unless you've been
where I am.

I don't want this to end.

Adam Strohschein

I love you.

"I love you...I do, I hate you...I do"

Adam Strohschein

Last night didn't even feel real, like
something from a movie or a song.
I don't know if I deserve this feeling,
do I?

One of my favorite things about us is our ability to slow time. Like our simply being together is this source of power we keep graviting towards. Never one without the other, forever infused.

I've never felt this good before.

When I'm with you, nothing else exists. It's just the two of us.

With you by my side nothing is impossible, every obstacle we cross only brings us closer together.

Adam Strohschein

I wish there was another way to tell you how much I love you, I don't feel like I can express it enough, with words or actions alone.

How did everything happen? One day we were complete strangers never knowing the other existed. Now we are inseparable.

Adam Strohschein

I can't help but study you. The way
you speak, the way your hands fit
perfectly in mine, your smell, your
taste.

Life was so confusing before you,
every step was one of blind faith never
truly knowing where I was heading.
But your light was always in the
distance, slowly growing with each
step I took, every hurdle I overcame to
reach you.

I finally made it and it's everything I
had hoped it'd be.
If this is a dream, may I never wake.

Adam Strohschein

Every moonlit room.

Every embrace.
Every single dance in the dark that we shared is something I selfishly enjoy whenever I need it, and I don't care.

I've never openly enjoyed that statement as much as I do now.

You calm the storm within.

Adam Strohschein

I could sit with you for hours not doing anything, just being with you is relaxing.

I love you,
I do.

Adam Strohschein

Laying in bed and talking about anything and everything with you is something I could do forever.

You bring out my goofy side, we become two children exploring the world like it's our playground.

Adam Strohschein

I don't think we've ever watched a movie all the way through, to be honest I like the ending we act out more.

I crave you

thirst for you

your taste is delicious

your smell is intoxicating.

I can never get enough of you.

I'm addicted

and I want more.....

Little do we realize it or not.

We are both creating a world.

Filled with codewords, a language only we understand.

Memories.

And healing all from within.

The courage you give me to be my true self is something I've never felt with anyone else......Do I deserve this?

Adam Strohschein

Exploring you physically and mentally
is my favorite.

Late night drives with you are a part of our healing, we can be vulnerable.
It's just us and the night.

Adam Strohschein

Sometimes you drive me crazy
sometimes we fight,
we laugh,
we cry.
We aren't even two people anymore
we act as one.
I can't imagine myself without you.

Don't let this good story come to a close we have so many stories to live, to tell, to laugh and remember forever.

Let's go out there and give them a show.

One they will inspire to be.

Adam Strohschein

I feel sometimes you're holding back
from fully letting me in. I offer my
entire self to you, every inch,
imperfection,
dream,
fear,
every
single
thing.

For you

only you.

Please let me in.

Adam Strohschein

I want to know all of you.

You're my therapy.

My insecurities found their way back and hurt you, I never wanted them to, I'm not perfect, I make mistakes. I cannot express my regret enough. Along with bringing out the good in me, you also have full access to the bad.

I'm sorry.

I've let you down.

Adam Strohschein

Thank you for being patient with me. I'm trying my best and I can't tell you enough how much I appreciate everything.

You're the type of person that inspires artists to create.

You are art.

Beauty at all angles.

Sometimes you get real nasty with me, your words and actions don't match whom I fell in love with. And sometimes I wonder if maybe I made a mistake. I don't want to think this way, but you know how to cut me deep and the wounds take longer to heal each time.

Your energy is different around me.

Something is wrong.

Please don't let what I'm thinking to be true.

Adam Strohschein

I don't know what to say or even think right now.

"I love you...I do, I hate you...I do"

Why?

I'm so numb.

You look really good when you lie.

Adam Strohschein

I hope everything was worth it.

I let you in and you destroyed me, I let
my guard down.

Adam Strohschein

I hope you hurt as much as I do, so you can feel what you've done to me.

Did you even mean anything you told me? How could a person say some of the most beautiful, reassuring words I've ever heard and then say some of the most hateful, hurtful ones I've ever heard.

Adam Strohschein

Somedays I sleep all day,

others I can't at all.

Please make this feeling go away
I can't take it anymore.

I'm completely drained.

Every day I find myself thinking about you.

I don't know how to move on from you, I invested so much of my time and energy into you.

Maybe I was in love with the idea of you.

Adam Strohschein

I don't know what I'm doing.

What is wrong with me? Didn't I say and do the right things? I'm not perfect by any means and I never claim to be but did I deserve any of this?

Adam Strohschein

I became so addicted to you that when
things ended the withdrawal was
unbearable.

Heard you moved on already.

That was quick.....

Adam Strohschein

I should've never let you in.

I should have just walked away before it started.

I should've never let you get close.

I'm so numb.

Adam Strohschein

.

I hate you.

I HATE YOU.

Adam Strohschein

I hate you. I hate you I hate
you I hate you I hate you I
hate you I hate you I hate
you I hate you I hate you I
hate you I hate you I hate
you I hate you I hate you I
hate you I hate you I hate
you i hate you I hate you I
hate you I hate you I hate
you I hate you I hate you I
hate you I hate you I hate
you I hate you I hate you i
hate you I hate you I hate
you I hate you I hate you I
hate you i hate you I hate
you I hate you I hate you I
hate you i hate you i hate
you i hate you I hate you I
hate you I hate you I hate
you I hate you I hate you I
hate you I hate you I hate
you I hate you I hate you I
hate you I hate you I hate
you I hate you I hate you I
hate you I hate you I hate
you I hate you I hate you I
hate you I hate you I hate
you I hate you I hate you I

hate you I hate you I hate
you I hate you I hate you I
hate you I hate you I hate
you I hate you I hate you I
hate you I hate you I hate
you I hate you I hate you I
hate you I hate you I hate
you I hate you I hate you I
hate you I hate you I hate
you I hate you I hate you I
hate you I hate you I hate
you I hate you I hate you I
hate you I hate you I hate
you I hate you I hate you I
hate you I hate you.

You liar

you cheater

you manipulator.

I fucking hate you.

117

Adam Strohschein

How dare you, <u>seriously</u> how
fucking dare you come into my
life and let me into your life
and then you destroy me like you
don't even care.

I hope you experience exactly
what you did to me and I hope
you live the way I'm currently
feeling every single day. I hope
you lose trust. I hope you feel
the pain. I hope you cry at the
thought of me. I hope my
presence brings you regret. I
hope it tears you up inside. I
want you to go away, I don't
want to see or hear about you
ever again.

Adam Strohschein

Whenever people mention your
name, my whole body becomes
numb. Even your name still
evokes a reaction in me,
I hate it.

How can you just go about your day like nothing happened? How can you live with the fact you destroyed another human with your words and actions? Do you even feel?

Adam Strohschein

I'll show you.

You'll never find someone like me, you'll only find pieces here and there in someone else.

I'm irreplaceable.

I hate who I've become, what I
let you get away with.

If I never saw you again that'd
be just fine.

Adam Strohschein

I feel guilty whenever friends
or family are around me and I'm
just an empty shell of who I
was.
They care so much about me,
When I care so little for
myself.

I hate when people tell me
"You'll find someone else"
I don't want "someone" else.
I want what we had.
I want you.

Adam Strohschein

As much as people would be
disappointed with me, if you
wanted to work things out.
I'd come running back in an
instant.

I hate how much of a hold you
have on me.

Whenever a song comes on that
reminds me of you.

I turn it off.

Do you know how many songs you
ruined for me?

Adam Strohschein

There are so many things

I want to tell you.

So many stories.

Music you'd love.

Movies you'd enjoy.

And it tears me up knowing I can't
tell you.

You're not there anymore…..

I'm mourning the loss of someone
who isn't dead.

Adam Strohschein

Whenever I'm with someone else it's scary to realize they don't know what my favorite things are, my birthday, what makes me angry or upset. I go through the motions with them, just hoping to feel a small piece of what you gave me. But it's not fair to them.

Who have I become?

I blamed myself for everything,
asking "What's wrong with me?"
when I should have been asking
"what's wrong with you?"
I put you so high on a pedestal
that you could never be held
accountable for your actions,
that's what was wrong with me.

For a while everything in my day redirected back to you as a constant reminder, but as time went on.

I found myself not thinking about you.

Till one day.

I didn't at all.

Adam Strohschein

It happened in an instant.

Adam Strohschein

Like when we met, in an instant.

You'd like who I'm with now, they are a lot like you in ways.

But just as I stated "I'm irreplaceable" you as well were irreplaceable. One of a kind were the moments we shared, the quiet, the tears, the laughter, the embraces, the vulnerability, the intimacy, the world we both created together and lived in is something I will forever look back on in moments when I need it most.

One of a kind.

I tried to hate you
for what you did to me.
But as time passed and I looked back I
realized you were like my favorite book,
one I read and dived into when I needed it
most. I became so intertwined with it I lost
sight of myself, so lost in your character my
own storyline ceased to progress. That's
not your fault it's mine. The next person to
pick up your book is going to treasure it as
much as I did. So much so they might not
be able to put it down. I wanted to renew it,
believe me I did. But I'm different now, I can
look back in a nostalgic light. You will
always forever hold a place in my library.

Adam Strohschein

You were my greatest lesson.

Adam Strohschein

Author Note

Love is one of the most sought-after
feelings, the need to be wanted, to be
appreciated for all your faults and
successes unconditionally without
judgement to just be who you are.
We fight for it
sacrifice for it
steal for it
lie for it
completely change for it.
All for this single emotion. We have been
conditioned into believing you need
someone else to feel it, before you can
love another you must find it from
within, and from there it will find you.

Adam Strohschein

Haley Sharon creates art designs under the name "Omystickers" on Redbubble.

Check out other books from "Gently Insert This Into Your Life" Publishing.

Adam Strohschein